Just
Walk
Across
the
Room

Also by Bill Hybels

Becoming a Contagious Christian
(with Mark Mittelberg and Lee Strobel)
Courageous Leadership
Descending into Greatness (with Rob Wilkins)
Fit to be Tied (with Lynne Hybels)
Honest to God?
Rediscovering Church (with Lynne Hybels)
The Volunteer Revolution

The New Community Series
(with Kevin and Sherry Harney)

Colossians

James

1 Peter

Philippians

Romans

The Sermon on the Mount 1

The Sermon on the Mount 2

The InterActions Small Group Series
(with Kevin and Sherry Harney)

Authenticity	*Love in Action*
Character	*Marriage*
Commitment	*Meeting God*
Community	*New Identity*
Essential Christianity	*Parenting*
Fruit of the Spirit	*Prayer*
Getting a Grip	*Reaching Out*
Jesus	*The Real Deal*
Lessons on Love	*Significance*
Living in God's Power	*Transformation*

BILL HYBELS

WITH ASHLEY WIERSMA

Just Walk Across the Room

FOUR SESSIONS ON
SIMPLE STEPS
POINTING PEOPLE
TO FAITH

ZONDERVAN®

WILLOW
Willow Creek Resources

ZONDERVAN.com/
AUTHORTRACKER
follow your favorite authors

Just Walk Across the Room Participant's Guide
Copyright © 2006 by Bill Hybels

Requests for information should be addressed to:
Zondervan, *Grand Rapids, Michigan 49530*

ISBN-10: 0-310-27176-2
ISBN-13: 978-0-310-27176-5

Interior design by Beth Shagene

Printed in the United States of America

07 08 09 10 11 12 13 • 25 24 23 22 21 20 19 18 17 16 15 14 13 12 11 10 9 8

Contents

. . . . ●

Introduction

· · · · •

Shortly after Jesus' resurrection, he appeared to his disciples on a mountain in Galilee. The wide-eyed group sat with rapt attention as he delivered a few standing orders to be carried out until he returned. Remember what they were?

> "Go out and train everyone you meet, far and near, in this way of life, marking them by baptism in the threefold name: Father, Son, and Holy Spirit. Then instruct them in the practice of all I have commanded you."
>
> MATTHEW 28:18–20A, MSG

Immediately after recognizing what's commonly referred to as the "Great Commission," the next thought that crosses your mind (if you're like many Christians) is smothered with obligation ... or worse yet, with guilt. *I know I should be accomplishing the Great Commission, but I can't seem to get past that first word ... Go.*

We *go* all the time. We go to work, go home, go out to eat, go shopping, go to sporting events, go to bed. But something deep inside us knows that Jesus' "go" carries with it a very different connotation.

His "go" means our feet have to get unstuck from where they're currently planted. It means we have to agree to action. It means we have to accept a little risk and stick one foot in front of the other to engage with another human being ... having no idea where it all will lead.

A daunting task for some, to say the least.

Friends, if your desire to "go" and reach out to the people around you is strong, but you find yourself perpetually stuck in "stay" mode, this study is for you. Statistically, only 10 percent of *any* congregation would raise their hands if asked who has the formal gift of evangelism or who does any evangelizing on a regular basis. Which means there's a substantive number of believers sitting around you each weekend who are all locked up when it comes to pointing those outside the faith toward God.

Just Walk Across the Room: The Four-Week Experience is a campaign designed to raise the value of evangelism for everyone in your church. This means that at the end of four weeks' time, they will have a fresh understanding of what "evangelism" really means, as well as a dose of inspiration regarding how to get it done. In addition to having some unexpected fun this month, I think you'll come away from the experience anxious to "go" in ways you've never before dreamed.

One closing thought before you dive in: Jesus' mountaintop speech to the disciples that day didn't end with his memorable series of commands. Probably detecting a little nervous energy in the audience, he concluded things with a single promise (and aren't we all glad!):

> "I'll be with you as you do this, day after day after day, right up to the end of the age."
>
> MATTHEW 28:20B, MSG

As you work through the material over the coming weeks, remember that evangelism isn't something you have to "gear up" for. Fundamentally, evangelism is about submitting to God's agenda in a social situation, in a conversation, in your moment-by-moment life. And, like Matthew's gospel says, he will be with you every step of the way.

BILL HYBELS
Founding and Senior Pastor
Willow Creek Community Church

The Single Greatest Gift

· · · · ·

[Look to Jesus] Who, being in very nature God,
did not consider equality with God something to be used
to his own advantage; rather, he made himself nothing by taking
the very nature of a servant, being made in human likeness.
And being found in appearance as a human being, he humbled
himself by becoming obedient to death—even death on a cross!
PHILIPPIANS 2:6–8

BEFORE YOU MEET

1. Read the introduction and chapters 1 and 2 in the *Just Walk Across the Room* hardcover book.

2. Complete the "Simple Steps We All Can Take" activity introduced during the weekend worship service (see page 10 for details). NOTE: If you are using this small group curriculum outside of the *Just Walk Across the Room* four-week campaign, simply disregard any item with a footprint symbol beside it.

3. Begin praying for one or two people for whom you want to take a "walk across the room" during this four-week experience. Beginning on page 69 of this participant's guide, you'll find space to log your prayer requests and the answers you receive.

Simple Steps We All Can Take

If you are a Christ-follower, consider how *you* wound up in the kingdom of God. Most likely, your story involves someone, somewhere who took a risk to walk across a room in order to point you toward faith. Maybe they extended a hand of friendship or engaged you in conversation. Regardless of the details, the end result was you submitting your life to God. If you still maintain contact with this person, then fill out and mail your *"God Used You to Help Point the Way"* note of gratitude to him or her today.

If you're not in touch with this person any longer, you may instead choose to mail your card to someone who epitomizes what it means to be a walk-across-the-room person, actively living out their faith in their day-to-day lives.

BIG IDEA — *THE SINGLE GREATEST GIFT*

The single greatest gift Christ-followers can give to the people around them is an introduction to the God who created them, who loves them, and who has a purpose for their lives. Nothing beats it—not monetary gain, not job opportunities, not recognition or accolades. This is what evangelism is—constantly watching for ways to give that gift to someone living far from God.

SESSION ONE OVERVIEW

This week, as you view the story of Brian Anderson, a vice president with a development consulting firm in Chicago and former soccer coach for Bill Hybels' son, watch for:

- Why Christ's walk from heaven to earth is a model for us all
- How learning from the Master—Jesus Christ—can help you become a "walk-across-the-room" person starting today
- What it means to pay attention to and be led by spiritual promptings

 VIDEO OPENER (2 MINUTES)

Play the session one video opener on the *Just Walk Across the Room Four-Week Experience* DVD.

 ICEBREAKER (6 MINUTES)

Think of your favorite interest, hobby, or recreational activity. Who would you like to spend a day with in order to soak up their knowledge and expertise in this area? Why?

VIDEO TEACHING (15 MINUTES)

Play the session one teaching segment on the DVD. Use the space below for your notes.

Video Observations

GROUP STRIDES, PART A (31 MINUTES)

1. What part of Brian's story had the greatest impact on you? Please explain.

2. As you think back on your own journey toward God, who is the main person who "took a walk" for you?

3. How would you describe the way in which this person reached out to you?

What part of that experience was most affirming or encouraging to you?

4. Reflect on a time when you believe *you* helped point someone toward God. Perhaps you said to a friend, "I'll pray for you," or you invited a neighbor to a Christmas Eve service. How would you feel if you discovered that this person wound up putting their trust in Christ as a result of the spiritual impact you had on their life?

5. What does Luke 19:10 say about Jesus' mission in coming to earth?

"For the Son of Man came to _____

_____*."*

6. Jesus was crystal clear about how he was going to invest his days while he was here on earth. How might this reality have freed him up from the fears and insecurities we typically face when approaching the work of evangelism?

7. The Bible says that all Christ-followers can have the same confidence in their mission and access to the same power to fulfill it that Jesus had, because they have the Holy Spirit living inside of them. Take another look at the "Before You Meet" section of this week's study. When you were asked to begin praying for one or two people for whom you might walk across a room, who came to mind?

In what ways would your mission in life be supported if you were to take steps toward them?

8. Near the beginning of this week's teaching video, you heard Bill Hybels mention that he's talked to many people who have been "freaked out" by evangelism at one time or another. He offered several explanations as to why this was the case. Have any of these ever been true for you? Check any that apply.

☐ I feel like I have to master a massive amount of apologetics information.

☐ I think I have to have a different personality than God gave me.

☐ I truly believe that evangelism is a formidable challenge I could never rise to.

9. In this week's video, Bill Hybels made the statement that *the single highest value in the evangelistic endeavor is to be attuned to and cooperative with the promptings of the Holy Spirit.* How might this reality relax you as you prepare to take a few steps toward people living far from God?

VIDEO SUMMARY (2 MINUTES)

Play the session one summary on the DVD.

- Christ-followers take walks across rooms because Jesus Christ—the Master of evangelism—took a walk for them.

- Taking walks in this manner is what all Christ-followers were born to do, reaching out a hand of compassion, choosing to say a kind word, hoping to bestow the great gift of grace on anyone and everyone they meet.

- The key to "success" in evangelism is walking when the Spirit says to walk, talking when the Spirit says to talk, and falling silent when the Spirit tells you that you've said enough. *This is what it means to stay attuned to and cooperative with the movement of the Holy Spirit!*

 GROUP STRIDES, PART B (2 MINUTES)

What's one thing you might do or say this week to take the first step toward one of the people you mentioned in response to the first part of question 7? Be prepared to share your response as your facilitator closes your discussion time in prayer.

 PRAYER POINTS (2 MINUTES)

Wrap up your discussion time this week by sharing your action item from "Group Strides, Part B" above. (Don't feel obligated to share the name of the person.) Ask God to open a door that you'll be able to walk through, and that you will sense his promptings in fresh ways as you commit to staying attuned to his Spirit.

·   ·   ·   ·   •

INDIVIDUAL STRIDES

Complete this section on your own this week.

1. In this week's discussion, you reflected on the primary person who took a walk across a room for you. Now, spend a few
moments thinking through all of the people along the way who
helped point you toward faith in God. Write the names of each
person and a word or two that describes the type of impact each
person had. (For examples, between -10 and -8, you might write,
"Josh—gave me book on faith, or between -1 and 0, you might
write, "Sarah—prayed with me to receive Christ.")

Names/Description of Actions They Took

Vibrant walk with Christ	10	_____
		_____
	5	_____
		_____
	1	_____
		_____
Accepted Christ	0	_____
		_____
	-1	_____
		_____
	-5	_____
		_____
Relied on self	-10	_____

2. How much of the time were "formulaic" approaches used in moving you along the spectrum?

☐ None of the time

☐ Some of the time

☐ Almost every step of the way

3. Take a look at the passages below, matching the way in which Christ pointed each person to faith with the names on the left.

_____ Nicodemus
(John 3:1–3)

A. Affirmed his master's faith

_____ Saul (Acts 9:1–9)

B. Showed love by offering a hug

_____ Centurion's servant
(Luke 7:1–10)

C. Caused him to be blind for three days

_____ Little children
(Mark 10:13–16)

D. Shot straight: "You must be born again!"

4. The examples in question 3 reveal the fact that Christ himself used a variety of approaches when pointing people toward his Father. What does this tell you about the usefulness of letting the Spirit lead instead of forcing a stringent or predetermined formula on people in evangelistic situations?

On page 41 of *Just Walk Across the Room*, author Bill Hybels says that "many people begin their spiritual quest at a negative ten and that my role is to facilitate their movement to a negative eight. That's it. Two points on the spectrum, and a result that is still in negative territory! It used to discourage me, but at some point I began to accept the fact that the role I am supposed to play is ... well, the role I'm supposed to play."

5. Keeping in mind your own journey toward faith, do you believe that your role in someone's life might merely be to help him or her move *one tick* along the spectrum toward vibrancy and fullness of life in Christ?

   ☐ Yes   ☐ Maybe   ☐ No

6. This week, ask God to show you ways that you may have made evangelism a mechanical or formulaic endeavor in the past. Ask him to give you clear direction regarding how to reach out to people in your sphere of influence. As you close out your time this week, jot down your response to the following question:

   Why do you think it's so easy to fall into a pattern of treating people as evangelistic projects instead of tending to them as unique treasures of God?

Living in 3D

. . . . .

> "You are the salt of the earth.
> But if the salt loses its saltiness,
> how can it be made salty again?
> It is no longer good for anything,
> except to be thrown out
> and trampled underfoot."
> MATTHEW 5:13

BEFORE YOU MEET

1. Read chapters 3, 4, and 5 in the *Just Walk Across the Room* hardcover book.

2. Complete the "Simple Steps We All Can Take" activity introduced in the weekend worship service (see page 22 for details).

3. Continue praying for your "Brians" — the one or two people you desire to reach out to during this four-week experience.

Simple Steps We All Can Take

During the weekend message, you were asked to consider the "next steps" that people took in helping you find your way to faith in God. Most likely, you were inspired and humbled as you recounted various resources people placed in your hands, words of encouragement you received from Christ-followers who cared for you, and simple acts of kindness that helped you grow in your awareness of what it meant to be a Christian.

Sometime this week, with these "next steps" fresh on your mind and heart, jot down the names of the people in your life who don't yet know God. What are one or two appropriate next steps you might take in each of their lives to help them move a few ticks toward faith?

BIG IDEA — *LIVING IN 3D*

Effective, relationally based evangelism can only happen when Christ-followers are truly engaged in the lives of people around them. This means they choose to **D**evelop friendships, **D**iscover life stories, and **D**iscern appropriate next steps based on the Holy Spirit's promptings — in other words, live in "3D."

SESSION TWO OVERVIEW

This week's session brings to life the concept of living in 3D through the story of "Super" Dave Wright, one of Bill Hybels' sailing buddies. You'll discover how to:

- Place your emphasis on building a friendship instead of on "saving a soul"

- Leverage resources around you—including your time—to accomplish the work of evangelism

- Rely on the Holy Spirit to prompt you toward appropriate next steps

 VIDEO OPENER (2 MINUTES)

Play the session two opener on the *Just Walk Across the Room Four-Week Experience* DVD.

 ICEBREAKER (8 MINUTES)

Ready for a little Neighbor Trivia? See how you fare in completing the activity on pages 24 and 25. It makes no difference where you live—suburban neighborhood, city-center high-rise, apartment complex, or rural farm. Your small group facilitator will guide you through each aspect of the activity in turn.

DIRECTIONS:

1. Write the names of six of your current neighbors in the blanks provided, a neighbor per each house icon (extra credit for knowing kids' names too!).
2. Place a number beside each family representing how many years they've lived there.
3. Note what occupations are represented in each family.
4. Which of your neighbors are Christians? Draw a cross next to the names.
5. Circle the names of the people who have ever been inside of *your* home.
6. Place a star beside the ones with whom you've had meaningful conversation in the past month.

(Bob Smith)   Teacher
NAME   OCCUPATION

† Betty *   Office Assistant

† Billy

7   † Susan   † Kayla *
YEARS

---

†Cathy + Gary   Tool + Die
NAME   OCCUPATION

Jason

7 - 8
YEARS

Jim + Tami Ferguson install
NAME   OCCUPATION

Tyler + Dillon   Sprinkler

YEARS

Doug + Sue Williams   Consumers • Vet
NAME   OCCUPATION

_____
_____
YEARS _____

Jennifer + Todd   school social workers
NAME   OCCUPATION

_____
_____
YEARS _____

Cathy + Jim   DNR
NAME   OCCUPATION

_____
_____
YEARS _____

Wendy   Duman
NAME   OCCUPATION

_____
_____
YEARS _____

Nancy + David Worden

VIDEO TEACHING (15 MINUTES)

Play the session two teaching segment on the DVD. Use the space below for your notes.

Video Observations

GROUP STRIDES, PART A (30 MINUTES)

Develop Friendships

1. Sometimes, the longer people walk with Christ, the fewer their interactions with people living far from God. They become "cocooners"—men and women who rarely step outside of their warm, safe, comfortable Christian circles. But for other Christians, the opposite is true: over time, they experience an *increase* in their love quotient for people outside the faith, making them more of a "connector." How have you seen the cocooning pattern or the connecting pattern occur in your own life?

2. *Developing friendships* means Christ-followers stay intentional about rubbing shoulders with people far from God, with the hope of helping point them toward faith. When you notice yourself veering toward a cocooning pattern, what are some ways for you to move toward connecting again?

Discover Stories

3. In what ways can you relate to various aspects of "Super" Dave's story? Several of them are listed below to jog your memory.

   • Negative religious experiences during adolescent years

   • Witnessed a close friend submitting their life to Christ

   • Significant loss—for Dave, it was the death of his father

   • Lengthy journey to faith in God

4. Once you make the decision to connect with people outside the faith, as Bill did with Dave, why is it so important to understand their stories before trying to engage in spiritual discussions with them?

Discern Next Steps

5. On page 97 of *Just Walk Across the Room*, Bill Hybels says that, "everyday, seemingly insignificant things can become divine, life-altering tools in the hands of compassionate Christ-followers." What role did the following "everyday things" play in Dave's journey toward God?

   • Books/tangible resources

   • Time

   • Recreational interests

6. The simple expression of a heartfelt emotion also played a pivotal role in helping Dave come to faith in Christ. How did it strike you when Bill told Dave, "I'm not going to heaven without you, Supe"?

How does this comment reflect a "bottom-line value of love" toward Dave?

Have you ever felt this way toward someone in your own life? If so, did you tell them about it? Why or why not?

 VIDEO SUMMARY (1 MINUTE)

Play the session two summary found on the DVD.

- Over time, most Christ-followers drift into a cocooning pattern rather than intentionally connecting with people who are living far from God.

- Jesus' dream is that all of his followers would become walk-across-the-room people who focus outwardly, love radically, and lay awake at night *consumed* with thoughts of how to point people toward faith in God.

- Living in 3D means deciding to engage; discovering other people's stories; and discerning appropriate next steps in spiritual conversations.

GROUP STRIDES, PART B (2 MINUTES)

1. Think about one of your "Brians." What stage of living in 3D do you think you're in with this person right now? Place your "Brian's" name in the top blank, and check the box below that corresponds to the stage of 3D living that you're presently experiencing with this person. Then, jot down a few thoughts in response to that item's follow-up question.

   My "Brian": _____

   ☐ Develop friendships—We're just now establishing common ground.

   How can I continue to practice a "bottom-line value of love" toward this person, regardless if they ever make a faith decision or not?

   ☐ Discover stories—I'm in the process of unearthing his or her life's story.

   What is one question I could ask to understand their life's journey better?

   ☐ Discern next steps—I've taken a few steps to help this person find faith in God.

   What resources is God prompting me to provide for this person, such as a book or a CD, a listening ear, or a few hours engaged in a shared recreational activity?

PRAYER POINTS (2 MINUTES)

Regardless of which stage of 3D living you find yourself in, the relationships that already exist in your life can serve as fertile ground for God to do some serious seed-sowing through you. Ask him for clarity as you assess which stage you're in; ask for wisdom as you seek to point people toward him; and ask for guidance as you take action.

*   *   *   *   •

INDIVIDUAL STRIDES

Complete this section on your own this week.

The Message paraphrase of Matthew 5:13 reads: "Let me tell you why you are here. You're here to be salt-seasoning that brings out the *God-flavors* of this earth. If you lose your saltiness, how will people taste godliness? You've lost your usefulness and will end up in the garbage" (emphasis added).

God-flavor. You probably won't find that one at your local ice cream shop, but its residue can be just as sweet. Think of it: evangelism doesn't have to be any harder than bringing out the God-flavors of the people around you each and every day.

1. Take a look at your relational circles. Where is your impact the most "God-flavored" and where is it blandest? Mark your responses with an X on the continuums below.

	Bland	God-flavored
My family		
My circle of friends		
My recreational groups		
Among people I don't know		
My church community		
My coworkers		
My neighborhood		

2. Why do you suppose it's easier to be "God-flavored" in certain environments than in others?

3. Take another look at your neighborhood diagram from this week's "Icebreaker" segment. In your quest to bring out the God-flavors of the people right around you, what is one way you can reach out to a neighbor this week?

On page 67 of *Just Walk Across the Room*, Jesus is described as having "an uncanny ability to look past the obvious flaws in people's lives and envision who they could become if the power of God were released in their lives. Intrinsically, he just *wondered* about people. Wondered what they could become. Wondered how they might look in a transformed state. Wondered what impact they could have if their lives were invested in things of eternal value."

4. When was the last time you stopped in the middle of a busy day and simply *wondered* about someone you came across? Perhaps you were standing in a line and struck up a conversation with the guy in front of you; or maybe you were rushing out of a meeting but took the time to *really* ask how a coworker was doing. Describe your experience below.

5. How do you suppose *wondering* about people's lives correlates to accomplishing the work of evangelism?

6. Read Psalm 139, paying special attention to verse 14, which says that all people are "fearfully and wonderfully made." This week, choose *one day* to live with a Psalm 139 attitude. With each person you come across, remind yourself that God orchestrated every personality trait, crafted every competency, and engineered every physical feature you see. At the end of your "Psalm 139 day," log your thoughts below regarding the power of treating people as marvelous, God-architected creations.

The Power of Story

. . . . ●

Always be prepared to give an answer
to everyone who asks you to give the reason
for the hope that you have.
1 PETER 3:15B

BEFORE YOU MEET

1. Read chapters 6, 7, and 8 in the *Just Walk Across the Room* hardcover book.

2. Complete the "Simple Steps We All Can Take" activity introduced in the weekend worship service (see page 38 for details).

3. Continue praying for your "Brians." Have you seized an opportunity to say a word or reach out a hand to one or more of these people? Note your experience on your Prayer Requests & Answers pages.

Simple Steps We All Can Take

Have you already written down your before-and-after faith story? If so, go ahead and email it to the address given to the congregation during weekend services. The feedback will only sharpen your articulation of what God has done in your life.

If not, stop everything and get it done now! You might just have the opportunity to share it this week—in the heat of that moment, you'll be so glad you went through the paces of thinking through your story, getting it down on paper or screen, and sending it off for some objective input.

Remember, no "Hephzibahs" or "Beulahs" in your before-and-afters ... no "look at me, I'm Super-Christian" ... no eighteen-page renditions, deal? Keep it brief, humble, easy to understand, and real.

BIG IDEA — *THE POWER OF STORY*

Regardless if they are formally "gifted" in evangelism or not, all Christ-followers can be prepared to engage people in spiritual conversations and do what they can to point people toward faith in God. When conversations take a spiritual turn, it is critical to know how to convey two stories with humility, clarity, and brevity: your own faith story and God's good news story.

SESSION THREE OVERVIEW

Have you ever thought about what makes a bad story bad? This week, through humorous skits, you'll learn firsthand what *not* to do when sharing your faith story. Elements include:

- Acting as if you're superior to your listener
- Being unclear
- Speaking in "religionese"
- Droning on and on

Then, in hopes of infusing you with the *right* way to do things, you will hear several well-told faith stories—evidence of God's intervention in people's lives—articulated with clarity, brevity, and humility.

 VIDEO OPENER (2 MINUTES)

Play the session three opener on the *Just Walk Across the Room Four-Week Experience* DVD.

 ICEBREAKER (2 MINUTES)

Think of a *brief* story regarding something that has significantly impacted your walk with Christ. Perhaps you or someone you know overcame a devastating loss ... or experienced unparalleled joy during a time of unusual blessing. What is the story, and what has been the impact on your spiritual journey?

VIDEO TEACHING (15 MINUTES)

Play the session three teaching segment on the DVD. Use the space below to take notes.

Video Observations

GROUP STRIDES, PART A (30 MINUTES)

1. In this week's video segment, you witnessed the telling of several really bad stories:

   - The **Long-winded** Story that went on ... and on ... and on ...
   - The **Fuzzy** Story that never seemed to get to the point
   - The **Religionese** Story that was laden with Christian insiders' jargon
   - The **Superiority** Story that was filled with pious, haughty language

   Which one bothered you the most and why?

2. On the other end of the spectrum, what are a few common denominators you noted in the "good stories" that were told at the end of the video segment?

   When a person is open to hearing your faith story, all that he or she really wants to know is what you were like *before* you met Christ; how you came to know Christ; and what you've been like *after* submitting your life to him. In other words, your personal "before-and-after." *This* is fundamental to what makes a faith story good!

3. In chapter 6 of *Just Walk Across the Room*, several examples are
   given of men and women from Scripture who had before-and-
   after experiences. Draw a line connecting each person to his or
   her faith story below:

Man who was born with a disability	"I walked in shame, but now I walk in grace!"
Zacchaeus, a wealthy tax collector	"I'd devoted myself to killing followers of Christ, but now I am a devoted one myself."
The apostle Paul	"I was gripped by greed, but now I'm gripped by the needs of the poor."
Woman who was caught in adultery	"I was blind, but now I see!"

4. Have a member of your group read 1 Corinthians 2:14–16 out
   loud. Based on these verses, why is it important for Christ-followers to tell their faith-stories in a manner that is simple, succinct,
   humble, and clear to people who are spiritually unconvinced?

Your "Before"

Just like the biblical characters noted in question 3, you have a "before-and-after" faith story. The following sections will help you craft your personal faith story. Work through questions 5–8 with a partner from within your small group.

5. What type of person were you before you met Christ? On the lines below, write down five to ten adjectives that come to mind. (If you came to faith at a young age, consider how you would describe what you were like prior to developing a thriving, more mature relationship with Christ.)

_____   _____

_____   _____

_____   _____

_____   _____

_____   _____

6. From the adjectives you noted in question 5, what is the one word in particular that best summarizes your "before" state? Write it here:

_____

Your Encounter with Christ

7. Now describe the circumstances that caused you to submit your life to Jesus Christ. What life-stage were you in? What input did you receive that finally triggered your desire to ask Christ into your life? What was the most significant thing about your making this decision?

Your "After"

8. Now, completing the sentence below, note the *primary difference* that Christ has made in your life.

   Since inviting Christ into my life, I've become _____

   _____

   _____.

9. Ready to tell your tale? Have a member of your group keep time as you tell your before-and-after story now. (One thing to keep in mind: in addition to conveying the basic before-and-after framework, be sure to mention one or two areas of your life that Christ is still refining. Nobody has "arrived" — it's important to acknowledge this reality.)

.   .   .   .   •

Not only is it critical for Christ-followers to know how to tell their stories well, but it is also important to be able to share God's redemptive story. As a group, view the extra segment in session three on the DVD that features Bill Hybels explaining three effective illustrations to use when conveying God's story.

 ## GOD'S REDEMPTIVE STORY (7 MINUTES)

Play the extra segment in session three on the DVD. Use the following space to take notes, if you wish.

GROUP STRIDES, PART B (2 MINUTES)

To get better at telling God's story, select one illustration from the list below to practice on your own this week. (For complete explanations of each illustration, read pages 135–138 in *Just Walk Across the Room*.)

☐ The Bridge

☐ "Do" vs. "Done"

☐ The Morality Ladder

 VIDEO SUMMARY (1 MINUTE)

Play the session three summary on the DVD.

• Every Christ-follower has a "before-and-after" story to tell; the goal is learning to tell it effectively.

• A well-told personal faith story leaves the listener feeling engaged and honored.

• A well-told personal faith story gives God the glory and leaves the door open to share his story of redemption.

 PRAYER POINTS (1 MINUTE)

Thank God for giving each person a story that makes sense once it's viewed inside the larger context of his story. Pray that every Christ-follower going through this four-week experience would get serious about telling both stories well. Just imagine the impact Christians could have in this generation if we got bold about telling of the transformational work Christ has accomplished in our lives—and told it well!

• • • • •

INDIVIDUAL STRIDES

Complete this section on your own this week.

Telling Your Story

1. One of the best ways to hone your personal faith story is to hear *other* people's stories. Talk to a few of your Christian friends about their faith stories this week. Record what you learn in the space below.

2. After learning from several other people's stories, refine your own faith story as necessary. Then, practice telling it this week with a few believing friends or family members who are willing to rate your story (in a grace-filled environment, of course) on the following four criteria:

   • **Brevity** (you got it done in forty-five to sixty seconds)

   • **Clarity** (you focused on one clear message)

   • **Simplicity** (no "religionese")

   • **Humility** (you weren't pious or haughty)

   Once you are confident that your story meets the four criteria listed above, send it to the email address announced during weekend services.

Telling God's Story

3. At the end of your small group meeting, you were asked to select one illustration of God's story to work on this week. Select the illustration you chose, and then take a few minutes to draw it in the space below, explaining the various aspects of the illustration out loud as you go.

   ☐ The Bridge

   ☐ "Do" vs. "Done"

   ☐ The Morality Ladder

Ready to see how you did? Check your work against the illustrations from chapter 7 of *Just Walk Across the Room*.

Illustration	Begins on page
The Bridge	135
"Do" vs. "Done"	137
The Morality Ladder	138

As you explain God's story to people living far from him, keep this in mind: although people have varying degrees of risk-tolerance, it's *always* unnerving to reach out to someone in an attempt to point them toward faith in God. You just never know how things will turn out once you pick up that pen to draw a picture for a real person with real questions and concerns about Christianity.

But while you never know what God will do in your midst, one thing is certain: heaven is cheering wildly for you as you take the risk to become a walk-across-the-room person.

4. God may give you an opportunity today to draw the illustration you practiced earlier for a real, live, seeking person. How does this make you feel?

☐ I live for this kind of thing and can't wait to see what God will do!

☐ I've engaged in these conversations with people before, but it's been a while ... I'm a little nervous.

☐ Oh, no! What have I done to deserve that?!

5. Always remember that God promises to guide you and to speak through you each time you tell his story. All he asks is for you to remain pliable and available to further his kingdom-building purposes. Read Proverbs 3:5–6 below; then, write a brief prayer thanking God for the truth you find there.

> Trust GOD from the bottom of your heart; don't try to figure out everything on your own. Listen for GOD's voice in everything you do, everywhere you go; he's the one who will keep you on track.
>
> PROVERBS 3:5–6, MSG

Dear God,

_____

_____

_____

_____

_____

_____

_____

_____

_____

_____

_____.

Grander Vision Living

. . . . •

Be wise in the way you act toward outsiders;
make the most of every opportunity.
Let your conversation be always full of grace,
seasoned with salt, so that you may know
how to answer everyone.
COLOSSIANS 4:5–6

BEFORE YOU MEET

1. Read chapters 9, 10, and 11 in the *Just Walk Across the Room* hardcover book.

2. Complete the "Simple Steps We All Can Take" activity introduced in the weekend worship service (see page 52 for details).

3. If you have seized an opportunity to reach out to a "Brian" in your life over the past few weeks, note the outcome on your Prayer Requests & Answers pages. Otherwise, ask God for an open door in the coming days as you complete this four-week experience.

Simple Steps We All Can Take

Ready to party? Let the Matthew Party concept inspire and energize you instead of cause you undue anxiety. Trust the Holy Spirit to guide you in your selection of guests and your choice of conversation topics throughout the actual event.

As you gear up, keep in mind the tips you received during the weekend service:

1. Keep it simple. Your Matthew Party does not need to be elaborate or expensive.

2. Do what makes *sense* for you to do ... if you have a pool, consider a pool party. If you live near a park, consider an afternoon picnic. If there's an appropriate place to meet at your apartment complex, lean into that resource. Think through what works for your environment.

3. Get the ratio right. Be sure that your unconvinced friends are not outnumbered by your Christian friends. Be sure there are *fewer* Christ-followers at your Matthew Party than nonbelievers. Otherwise, your unbelieving friends may feel ganged up on! And once that happens, you will have an impossible time wooing them back again.

4. Thank God in advance for what he will do! Your small act of obedience in hosting a few friends in your environment might just be the difference of eternity for them.

BIG IDEA — *GRANDER VISION LIVING*

What is Grander Vision Living? It's allowing other pursuits to fall away in order to focus on the priority that is nearest to the heart of God: people. When you choose to pursue the Grander Vision, you will be partnering with God in the most magnificent mission imaginable: finding what's lost, restoring what's broken, and reclaiming what's his.

SESSION FOUR OVERVIEW

This week, you will be introduced to Jim Glas, a long-time friend of Bill Hybels who is still wrestling with issues of faith. When Jim invited Bill to attend weekly dinner parties at his home, Bill chose to leverage them as spiritual opportunities. You may have similar social situations that you can maximize, or you may wish to instigate a few of your own; either way, this session will reveal the power of the "Matthew Party" as a magnificent catalyst for personal evangelism.

 VIDEO OPENER (2 MINUTES)

Play the session four opener on the *Just Walk Across the Room Four-Week Experience* DVD.

 ICEBREAKER (8 MINUTES)

How can spiritual rituals similar to the one Bill Hybels described reestablish a person's desire to submit to God's agenda for their day?

VIDEO TEACHING (15 MINUTES)

Play the session four teaching segment on the DVD. Use the space below for notes.

Video Observations

GROUP STRIDES, PART A (30 MINUTES)

1. Have you ever thought that being a Christian necessarily meant that you had to become a "lifestyle referee" to the world around you? How did it strike you when Bill said Christ-followers are under *no* obligation to play such a role?

2. What do you think of the "Matthew Party" concept—an event where you invite a few Christ-followers, several seekers, and several people who want nothing to do with God—as presented in this session's video?

3. Whether or not you've ever been involved in a Matthew Party, what fears or concerns would you have about hosting one now?

4. Besides the "highs and lows" exercise employed by the group in
the video, what other methods could be used to invite meaningful conversation during a Matthew Party?

The hope in throwing a Matthew Party, as Bill Hybels mentioned
in the video, is that in the midst of a social atmosphere, something spiritual would ignite. Seeing this happen firsthand, you
will be reminded how crucial it is to tap into God's supernatural
power that's alive and well in the heart of every believer. The
stakes are simply too high in evangelistic situations to "go it
alone."

5. Based on the following verses, what do you learn about the Holy
Spirit's involvement in the life of the Christ-follower?

John 14:16–21

Acts 1:8

Romans 8:26–27

John 15:7 says that if you remain in Christ and his word remains in you, you may ask whatever you wish and it will be given you. You might think that since God has the power to grant you whatever you wish, he would *always* move dramatically in people's lives. But as was evidenced by Jim and Bill's decade-long friendship, God's timing and plans are often different from ours (see Isaiah 55:8).

6. How can Christ-followers cultivate God's degree of patience when it doesn't seem like any spiritual progress is being made in the lives of people they care deeply about?

7. Jim Glas mentioned in the video that the trust he and Bill forged in their relationship played a key role in Jim reopening his heart to spiritual dialogue. Based on what you have learned so far in this four-week experience, what are some ways you can build trust with people who are far from God, so that when things finally turn spiritual, they are confident that you have their best interest at heart?

VIDEO SUMMARY (2 MINUTES)

Play the session four summary on the DVD.

By definition, Christ-followers who choose to become walk-across-the-room people live all of life with the Grander Vision in mind—working, shopping, recreating, and partying with God's people-priority constantly on their radar. Even if their friends and family members don't seem initially receptive to spiritual dialogue, they pray believing that one day, perhaps because of their faithfulness to "take a walk," everyone they know and love will be compelled to submit their lives to Christ.

 GROUP STRIDES, PART B (2 MINUTES)

Thinking back on the importance of God's power in evangelistic situations, if the Holy Spirit is the highway that leads to this supernatural power, then the onramp is *prayer*: constant, fervent prayer. The impact of prayer throughout the Bible is undeniable: healing occurred, barren women bore children, wars were won, wisdom was increased, forgiveness was extended, strength was offered, God's judgment was stayed, and so on. When have you experienced proof of the power of prayer most significantly in your own life?

PRAYER POINTS (1 MINUTE)

Thank God for the reality of the "mind-blowing thing called grace" that all Christ-followers enjoy. Ask him to prompt you toward prayer every morning—prayers for open doors of opportunity—so that you can play a role in giving someone a marvelous before-and-after story.

* * * * *

INDIVIDUAL STRIDES

Complete this section on your own this week.

In chapter 10 of *Just Walk Across the Room*, Bill Hybels reminds you that "Matthew Parties don't have to be formal, expensive, elaborate, or perfectly orchestrated. They just have to *happen*." During the weekend message, you were encouraged to host a Matthew Party this month. Take a few minutes to determine what type of gathering makes the most sense, given your personality and your situation.

1. Matthew Parties can range from a pool party or outdoor barbecue to a group of people hanging out at a local coffee shop. List all of the possible Matthew Party formats you could envision hosting. Allow the following ideas to get you started:

 • Pool party
 • Outdoor barbecue
 • Holiday get-together (Christmas, New Year's, Valentine's Day, etc.)
 • Sports tournament (golf, basketball, bowling, etc.)
 • Picnic at a local park

 • _____
 • _____
 • _____
 • _____
 • _____
 • _____

On pages 197–198 of *Just Walk Across the Room*, Bill Hybels suggests three categories of guests to consider for your Matthew Party. Here's how he describes them:

> "I had invited about twenty people who were living extremely far from God, by their own admission. These men and women had never been to Willow before, had never been to my house before, and spiritually speaking would profess to be 'going it alone.'

> "To that group, I added about twenty people who were in the Seeker Slow Lane—the remedial class of Christianity, you might say. On the rare occasion when I would badger them mercilessly, they'd agree to come to Willow. But it was sporadic attendance at best, usually involving a fair amount of kicking and screaming on their part. Most of them had been to my house previously to attend other parties, and all of them knew I was 'working' on them, nudging them along the (very) slow path to God. Maybe they would step across the line of faith someday, but in my estimation, it was going to take some time. A *lot* of time.

> "In addition to the twenty or so people who were very far from God, and the twenty or so people who were in-progress types, I had sprinkled in a dozen or so very strong Christ-followers from Willow to mix it up a bit. The screening process for this group in particular had been intense! I knew I couldn't afford any overzealous types showing up. No truth vigilantes. No bounty hunters. Just normal, mature, relationally intelligent, open-hearted, radically inclusive people who understood how high the stakes were that night—after all, I was going to put them in a room with friends of mine who, apart from a bona fide miracle, would spend eternity apart from God."

2. Jot down a few names in each group as you continue thinking through your upcoming gathering.

Those living extremely far from God

_____   _____

_____   _____

_____   _____

_____   _____

_____   _____

Those in the "Seeker Slow Lane"

_____   _____

_____   _____

_____   _____

_____   _____

_____   _____

Devoted Christ-followers

_____   _____

_____   _____

_____   _____

_____   _____

3. What do you want to see God do as a result of your Matthew
   Party? In the space below, capture your thoughts about your specific "goal" for this event.

There is no better way to close out this four-week experience
than to commit anew to communicating with God through
prayer. Write out your personal requests of God after reading
each of the categories listed on pages 63–67. Then, be prepared
to see God move in miraculous ways as you devote yourself to
the work of evangelism!

*"First, God, that my worldview
would align with yours ..."*

Ask God to reveal to you what you really believe about issues of
ultimate reality. Be reminded that his kingdom agenda desires for *all*
people to come to faith in him and live with him forever. As you pray,
ask for his heart which beats for people to become your heartbeat as
well.

_____

_____

_____

_____

_____

_____

_____

*"Next, that I would truly believe
in the power of the gospel ..."*

Pray that he would renew your hope in the power of the gospel. Do
you really and truly believe that God's message — his plan of salvation
— can change people's forevers?

_____

_____

_____

_____

_____

_____

_____

"That you would open doors for me today ..."

Echo the apostle Paul's words from Colossians 4:3–4: "And pray for us, too, that God may open a door for our message, so that we may proclaim the mystery of Christ, for which I am in chains. Pray that I may proclaim it clearly, as I should."

_____

_____

_____

_____

_____

_____

_____

"That I would allow the Spirit to direct everything I do and say ..."

Be reminded that words carry meaning. Big meaning! Ask God to rein in your tongue. Ask him to remind you of the power you carry with your words. Ask him for more, more, more wisdom in this regard. As you lean into the power and direction of the Holy Spirit, pray that you will think, speak, and move in accordance with his design for each and every interaction you have.

_____

_____

_____

_____

_____

_____

_____

"That you would silence the voices of doubt ..."

Pray that God would silence the voices of doubt that seek to dishearten, dismantle, and destroy. Ask him to remind you that your evangelistic efforts are not a self-image booster. Pray that he would keep your intentions focused on *other* people, not seeking to fulfill something in you, but rather to fulfill the greatest something in them—their need for God. Let the words of 1 Corinthians 15:58 minister to you as you pray: "Therefore, my dear brothers and sisters, stand firm. Let nothing move you. Always give yourselves fully to the work of the Lord, because you know that your labor in the Lord is not in vain."

_____

_____

_____

_____

_____

_____

_____

"That I would persevere until the end . . ."

Pray that you would be willing to pay the price of time and energy, remembering the price Christ paid for you; and that the peace of Philippians 4:7 — peace that goes beyond human understanding — would flood your spirit. Pray that you would be open to being used in new and different ways to lead people to faith in him; and that other Christ-followers would play the role they are supposed to play in people's lives. Pray that hearts would melt, people would be changed, and heaven-bound eternities would be secured.

"Finally, that I would devote myself to being a walk-across-the-room person!"

Miraculous outcomes await Christ-followers who are prepared to be used by God in changing people's forevers. Tell God that you are ready to be an instrument for good. Ask him how he desires to magnetize people to his message of grace, using you as a mouthpiece. And pray that eternities would dramatically shift as a result of your simple steps pointing people toward faith.

_____

_____

_____

_____

_____

_____

Prayer Requests & Answers

. . . . •

Date	Request
Date Answered	Description

Date	Request
Date Answered	Description

Date	Request
Date Answered	Description

Date	Request
Date Answered	Description

Date	Request
Date Answered	Description

Date	Request
Date Answered	Description

Date	Request
Date Answered	Description

Date	Request
Date Answered	Description

Date	Request
Date Answered	Description

Date	Request
Date Answered	Description

Date	Request
Date Answered	Description

Date	Request
Date Answered	Description

Date	Request
Date Answered	Description

Date	Request
Date Answered	Description

Date	Request
Date Answered	Description

Date	Request
Date Answered	Description

Notes

Notes

WILLOW

Willow Creek Association

Willow Creek Association

Vision, Training, Resources for Prevailing Churches

This resource was created to serve you and to help you build a local church that prevails. It is just one of many ministry tools that are part of the Willow Creek Resources® line, published by the Willow Creek Association together with Zondervan.

The Willow Creek Association (WCA) was created in 1992 to serve a rapidly growing number of churches from across the denominational spectrum that are committed to helping unchurched people become fully devoted followers of Christ. Membership in the WCA now numbers over 10,500 Member Churches worldwide from more than ninety denominations.

The Willow Creek Association links like-minded Christian leaders with each other and with strategic vision, training, and resources in order to help them build prevailing churches designed to reach their redemptive potential. Here are some of the ways the WCA does that.

- **A2: Building Prevailing Acts 2 Churches—Today**—an annual two-and-a-half day event, held at Willow Creek Community Church in South Barrington, Illinois, to explore strategies for building churches that reach out to seekers and build believers, and to discover new innovations and breakthroughs from Acts 2 churches around the country.

- **The Leadership Summit**—a once a year, two-and-a-half-day conference to envision and equip Christians with leadership gifts and responsibilities. Presented live at Willow Creek as well as via satellite broadcast to over one hundred locations across North America, this event is designed to increase the leadership effectiveness of pastors, ministry staff, volunteer church leaders, and Christians in the marketplace.

- **Ministry-Specific Conferences** — throughout each year the WCA hosts a variety of conferences and training events — both at Willow Creek's main campus and offsite, across the U.S., and around the world — targeting church leaders and volunteers in ministry-specific areas such as: evangelism, small groups, preaching and teaching, the arts, children, students, women, volunteers, stewardship, raising up resources, etc.

- **Willow Creek Resources®** — provides churches with trusted and field-tested ministry resources in such areas as leadership, evangelism, spiritual formation, spiritual gifts, small groups, stewardship, student ministry, children's ministry, the use of the arts — drama, media, contemporary music — and more.

- **WCA Member Benefits** — includes substantial discounts to WCA training events, a 20 percent discount on all Willow Creek Resources®, *Defining Moments* monthly audio journal for leaders, quarterly *Willow* magazine, access to a Members-Only section on WillowNet, monthly communications, and more. Member Churches also receive special discounts and premier services through WCA's growing number of ministry partners — Select Service Providers — and save an average of $500 annually depending on the level of engagement.

For specific information about WCA conferences, resources, membership, and other ministry services contact:

Willow Creek Association
P.O. Box 3188
Barrington, IL 60011-3188
Phone: 847-570-9812
Fax: 847-765-5046
www.willowcreek.com

We want to hear from you. Please send your comments about this book to us in care of zreview@zondervan.com. Thank you.

ZONDERVAN.com/
AUTHORTRACKER
follow your favorite authors